CONTENTS

CHAPTER 1: Situational Awareness – An Introduction

CHAPTER 2: Identifying Environment Hazards

CHAPTER 3: Identifying People Hazards

CHAPTER 4: Becoming Externally Aware

CHAPTER 5: The Mindset

REFERENCES

CHAPTER 1

Situational Awareness – An Introduction

What is Situational Awareness or SA?

"Situational awareness or situation awareness (SA) is the perception of environmental elements and events with respect to time or space, the comprehension of their meaning, and the projection of their status after some variable has changed, such as time, or some other variable, such as a predetermined event." This is the textbook definition provided by the United States Coast Guard.

Don't let the above definition turn you away. In layman's terms, SA means to be aware of what is happening in your surroundings, how it may change over time, how it may impact you and lastly knowing what to do at various stages. I'll give you an example; let's say you are driving and suddenly are driver cuts you off. In this case, the driver gets so close to your car that now you have to maneuver to avoid him. Do you know if a car is directly behind you? If you slam on your brakes you may get rear-ended. Can you swerve to the left or right and then decelerate? You could, but are there cars directly next to you or in your blind spot? If you swerve you may strike those vehicles as well. Are you wearing your seatbelt? You should be.

As you can see from the perspective of a driver being situationally aware can mean the difference between making it to work on time or being involved in a fatal car accident.

How to Hone Your SA Mentality

SA is often described more as a mentality than a thing you do. However, I find that with everything, if you have habits or rituals in place they will ultimately hone your skill level. In my opinion I don't feel that SA is really any different. Practice makes perfect and there are a few things you can do to develops the habits that will lead to a clear picture and response to SA. Physical training, mental training, scenario training, and proper sleep. These practices may seem pretty straight forward as I'm sure your parents preached this to you on a daily basis (minus the scenario training) but the habits above are crucial to honing and improving you SA mentality.

Let's start with physical training. It's no secret that many in the security industry are, out of shape. This isn't necessarily because the industry attracts people of lower fitness standards, quite the opposite. What I find is that most start out in good shape and as their career progresses they tend to spend more time working, more hours on the clock, more bad eating choices and each day these little decisions add up. An out of shape body can impact your ability to respond emergency situations or you yourself may become a victim due to a heart attack, low blood sugar, or succumb to heat exhaustion. Unless you train your body to be ready for the rigors of the job your reaction and speed will degrade which will ultimately ruin your ability to have sharp SA.

So how do we conduct physical training? Well, I'm a realist now and know that not everyone has a lot of time to exercise so I want to give you a few tips that might simplify things. Firstly, stretch. No matter what always ensure you set aside some time to stretch before and after your duty station. Stretching is proven to improve flexibility in your joints and reduce your chances of injury. It will also release tension in your body reducing stress overall and improving your mood. Next is cardio. Don't have time to run? No problem. If you are a Security Officer on a roving patrol you have a chance to kick it into high gear, burn some calories in, and improve your muscle tone. Patrol faster, don't run, just walk faster. When you increase your walking speed you increase your heartbeat. This will increase the number of calories you burn in a day and it will improve blood flow in the body.

Never, ever, ever take the elevator. That's right you heard me. Firstly, if you work in security and you get stuck in the elevator than you must wait for someone to rescue you and that doesn't look very good.

Secondly, the stairs have huge potential for cardiovascular training and you need to take advantage of that. With each burning step of the stairs you are burning double the calories you would from just walking and you are building strong thigh muscles and calves which will help prevent you from early fatigue or help you lift someone atop your shoulders and carry them out of a burning building. So, don't avoid the stairs, look at them as an opportunity for extracurricular activity and step-on!

Along with a physical sweat you want to work up a cerebral sweat through mental training. Personally, I prefer reading to keep up my mental sharpness by reading and reading often. I know many of you would ask me what to specifically to read or what books to recommend but honestly, it's so difficult to say that one book would do you better than others. In this case I would recommend that you read a variety of things throughout your day and make a habit of it. On one hand, you could have a career manual or technical book like the one you are reading now. This will provide great resources and immediate practical application. On the other hand, you could be reading a fantasy novel, a novel about aliens or maybe even a biography of someone you find inspiring (George Washington is pretty awesome). Try reading a little bit of both during your day and don't forget to throw some current events in there with the news. Local news is best to start with then you can move to international news.

In terms of the news you choose to read I would recommend your local paper or local papers website so you know what is happening in your town, county, or province. This news will almost always be factual and tend to avoid political topics. International news is a whole other beast and it would be difficult to tell you to watch CNN, FOX, or MSNBC without showing my own political leaning. However, what I can say is that if you get serious about international news it's good to read a little bit of all of them. You will sometimes get a point of view from one that you did not get from the other or you may find on news stations view of the topic is more factual versus an opinion based piece. With this formula for reading both factual, professional development, and entertaining literature this will make you a more well-rounded person, a more mentally sharp person, and more capable of carrying on conversations.

The next step in honing your SA mentality is scenario based training. As I said earlier, train like you fight, fight like you train. The more you practice at doing something the better you become. As time permits during your work shift take the time to practice or even run through minor scenarios. Perhaps a grease fire in the kitchen of your office. How would you respond? What door would be the safest to enter through? How do you know it's safe to go through that door? Where does the nearest fire alarm pull station reside? Where is the nearest fire extinguisher and should you grab one before you enter the kitchen? All of these are important questions that you must answer and that you can practice while on patrol. This will make you faster and more effective in the event that the fire actually occurs. Let's try another common emergency in an office or corporate setting; what about a medical emergency? Is your First Aid, CPR, and AED card up to date? When was the last time you drilled for a medical emergency? When was the last time you practiced CPR, or wrapping a bandage on someone? I would recommend asking your supervisor to set some time aside to refresh you on these medical emergency items at least once per month or at a minimum once for every ninety days. This will help to ensure that you are ready to respond and have enough confidence to carry out any task set before you.

Another word that comes to mind when discussing scenarios is drills. Drills with your fellow security team are much more crucial than your own scenario training. The reason for this being is that your team also has a kind of unified SA that they must harness. For example, if you are operating in a team of two or more can you tell who will bring the right equipment? Are you aware of what each person in the team should be doing at certain points and can you assist or tow the line if they forget or fall behind? This kind of team SA builds comrade, trust, and respect for one another. Not only that but it ensures that no matter the emergency if one member of your team fails in their duty the others will quickly recognize that gap and quickly fill it.

Lastly, to hone your SA mentality, or to even have an active SA mentality you must acquire the proper amount of sleep. I already see most of you rolling your eyes and sighing at the thought of actually getting a decent night's rest. What I want you to do is take that doubt and place it to the side for a moment and really analyze your day. What time do you wake up in the morning? What time do you have to be at work? What time do you get home? How many hours do you have at home before you go to bed? After many years of working in the Security Industry I have learned that going to sleep at a dedicated time (if possible and you're not doing 24/7 coverage of a principal) is the best way to go. Take a look at the below two examples of time management for your day and then try to do one yourself. Are you tired all the time? Ok then, how do you schedule some more sleep? Do you need a little more energy during the day? Then where can you schedule in that thirty or sixty-minute workout?

0500 Wake Up

0530 Exercise

0630 Drive to Work

0730 Arrive at Work 15 or 30 Minutes
Early

1130 Start Lunch

1230 End Lunch

1700 Drive Home

1800 Arrive Home

1830 Dinner

1900 Free Time

2000 Free Time

2100 Sleep

Bottom line is, if you don't get enough sleep you will not be effective and if you are not effective your SA will be completely offset. You will make mistakes, you will not notice things you would normally notice, you will be incapable of predicting outcomes and you will be incapable of responding properly. Again, I challenge you to map out your day, schedule your time, use it wisely, find shortcuts and create ways of using your time more efficiently. We all put on our pants the same way, we all have the same number of hours in a day. It doesn't matter if you are the CEO or the Security Officer. What matters is how you plan your day, how you utilize those minutes, how you utilize every second of every day.

There is probably a dozen or more factors that Security Professionals would point out that could improve or impact your SA level. I merely tried to cover those that I felt were core to SA and would have the greatest level of impact. If this is the first time you have read about SA and really spent time thinking about it then I would suggest you start with the items I mentioned above.

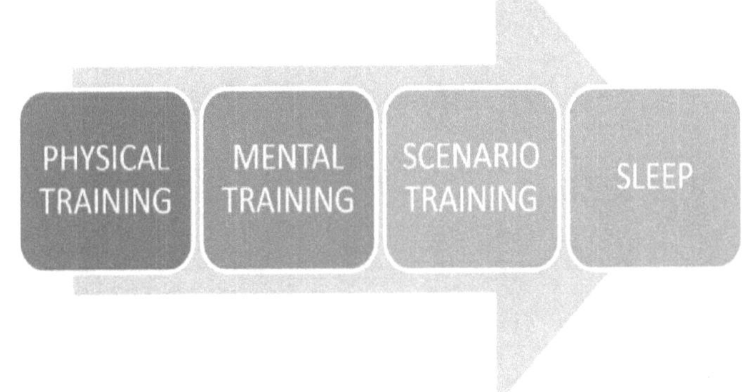

CHAPTER 2

Identifying Environment Hazards

There's a handy chart I like to utilize when talking about hazards and SA in your environment. See below;

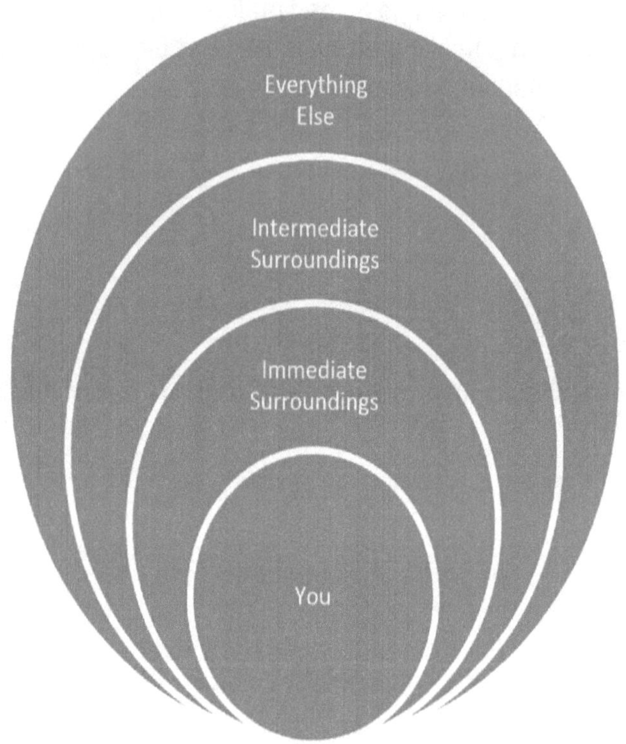

You

Believe it or not you need to be capable of maintaining SA of yourself and not just your surroundings. A great example is what you will do in response to aggression and are you currently capable of responding to aggression? Are you rested? Are you physically fit? All of these will come into play. If you are working a Security post where you are required to physically restrain individuals are you in the proper mental and physical condition to do so? How well do you know your body? After many years in this industry I know my aches and ticks, I know when I'm ready to get in it and I know when it's time to sit out. If you have a few chronic injuries, make sure you have a physical treatment regimen in place to either resolve them or mitigate the level of pain you experience.

What about your equipment? Do you have SA of all the equipment you utilize and its current condition? Did you test your radio before going on patrol? Is your radio battery fresh? Are you carrying a spare battery? If you don't do any of those things it will be difficult to call for help when you need it. What about your flashlight? Crimes occur mostly at night because of the element of concealment is on the criminals side. When you hear a loud noise are you just going to wander into the dark and become a victim or are you going to ensure your flashlight is ready to go and is capable of blinding and disorienting a possible assailant? Do you wear body armor? Have you kept it clean and dry? Are cracks beginning to form in the fabric after years of use? What is the recommended use limit for your armor? Will it be capable of stopping a bullet? These are the kinds of questions you should be asking yourself over and over again. If you can't maintain SA of yourself, it will be nearly impossible to respond to your immediate surroundings with defective gear. Know yourself, know your gear, test yourself, test your gear.

Immediate Surroundings

Your immediate surroundings include anything and everything beyond your physical self that are within a range that may impact you physically or mentally. It's difficult to give you a range of how aware your SA should be in your immediate surroundings but let me give you some examples and we can break it down from there.

The room you may be in will obviously have a significant impact on you and require a high level of SA. Are there others in the room that may harm you? Are there dangerous objects such as a utility transformer or even hazardous chemicals? Depending upon the situation these people and things can have an impact on you and your SA of your immediate surroundings needs to be high. In the immediate surroundings, you will have seconds or even just a fraction of a second to respond to a situation. What about cars or heavy objects around you? Are you working at a factory or warehouse? Accidents do happen and unfortunately Security Professionals become injured from time to time because they don't notice the forklift coming at them or the heavy unbalanced stack of boxes ready to topple over on them.

We talked about hazards indoors but what about outdoors? Perhaps it's a stormy day and as you leave your site you step into a puddle. Is there a downed powerline in the area? Is the water electrified? Are you wearing the proper safety shoes to help insulate you from electrical currents?

Intermediate Surroundings

Intermediate surroundings are those things that are within sight or nearby but do not have an immediate impact. Standing your post at a guard shack for example you could see a vehicle some distance away that suddenly takes a sharp turn at your parking lot. Because of your level of SA, you already recognized this vehicle barreling down the road giving your subconscious mind time enough to prepare possible worst case scenarios and how you may respond. As the vehicle raging down the may drive you immediately activate road blocks, step back from the guard shack to give yourself an evacuation route and radio or call into your security office the pending situation that is about to unfold. Suddenly the vehicle stops, the man inside is playing loud music, rolls down his window as your heart skips a beat he suddenly displays his drive on I.D. to enter the facility. It's Dave, the IT guy…

Everything inside or you, every single instinct was telling you that something was very wrong. As your heart beat and adrenaline begin to level off you start to feel silly, you shake it off and start to wonder why you were worried in the first place. What are the odds of something bad happening anyway? But that's just the point, isn't it? You see, it could have gone wrong, it could have gone as wrong as wrong can go. What if the driver of the vehicle didn't stop, what if he plowed right through the guard shack, or instead of displaying his I.D. in a fraction of a second what if it was a firearm? He could be a disgruntled current/former employee come to start an active shooter situation bent on claiming as many lives as possible.

It's important not to shake off these feelings of suspicion and danger. Your gut instinct has been developed over hundreds of thousands of years by ducking pterodactyls, out running grizzly bears, or knowing when someone was watching you in the woods. You need to trust these feelings and recognize the signs of when something is not right. Your SA can very well save you in the Intermediate surroundings by giving you those ample seconds or minutes to run scenarios through your mind and plan how you will respond to the threat when it arises. Dave the I.T. guy may have been just a harmless though irresponsible player in this episode but it could have been something else altogether.

Everything Else

Now that we have covered SA for you, your immediate surroundings and your intermediate surroundings let's take a moment to discuss everything else. There are things beyond your immediate visual and audible abilities to pick up and you need to be aware of what those may be. For example, Hurricanes. Do you keep up with the news? Do you work or live in a geographic area where hurricanes frequently occur? Than you will need to pay attention to the SA of everything else. Hurricanes are often days in the making giving local authorities ample time to ramp up a response and most importantly provide a communication to those who may be impacted so they can better prepare or evacuate early. Your local newspaper or local news television station will often provide this information so you can be aware of the thing you cannot see or feel but can be keenly aware that it is coming and it will impact you.

Another great example is Law Enforcement For Official Use Only (FOUO) briefings. These briefs often provide intelligence or information on situations the police have or are currently dealing with.

These can provide keys lessons learned to persons not yet familiar with these situations and how they could use the information to better protect themselves. A great example is super soakers or water pistols. Yes, these fun-loving toys have been used for decades by children and adults alike for entertainment and as a way to cool off during the hot summer months. Would it surprise you to say that on multiple occasions adult have used these toys to disguise real firearms? Take a look at the photo below.

Just a little frightening, right? To think that someone could take something so seemingly harmless such as a child's toy and convert it into a deadly weapon. This is in fact not the first time something like this has happened and it won't be the last. Now I want you to picture yourself on patrol on a hot summers day. You spot several teenagers, nearly young men, walking down the street near your campus or site and one of them is carrying a super soaker or large squirt gun. Would you be suspicious? Would you even for a moment think that perhaps this group of men have ill intentions and are in fact planning to assault you? Probably not, but these are the kinds of scenarios I want you to start baking in the oven of your mind. You need to raise your SA if you are going to survive these occurrences.

CHAPTER 3

Identifying People Hazards

The most unpredictable and dangerous thing you will deal with in your career is people. Now, let me insert a caveat by saying it's not just the people you think it may be. I need you to throw away stereotypes of what kind of people you might "think" are dangerous and I need you to expand your SA, expand your mind. Everyone, and I mean everyone, is capable of violence. What's the first thing you hear from witnesses after an active shooter situation? *He/She just snapped*, or, *He/She seemed like such a nice person*. Now don't get me wrong, there are general stereotype bad guys out there but what I'm trying to convey is that I do not want you to discount that nice lady you see every morning at the office, or the polite young man that nods his head every time he walks past you. As human beings, we are terribly complex with vast layers of emotions and life problems that ultimately impact how we interact with society.

Signals of Violence

Not everyone will display cues that they are about to commit violence and to that point if they do than no two people are the same. I'm going to tell you what you need to keep your eyes and what you need to look out for in the general sense that may help save your life.

Approaching or Being Approached By Unknown Persons

The hands do not lie. Humans were born with hands and poseable thumbs which some I think have correctly theorized helped to make us a smarter and more cunning mammal than the rest. This also makes us more dangerous. Earlier this year I went to the Zoo with my family and sat in front of many large animals including the silverback gorilla. I was in awe of this creatures utter size in comparison to me, its muscle mass, teeth and enormous hands. A human in one to one combat stood no chance against such a creature. Then I thought further back,

Neanderthals were up against creatures of even greater size and strength and yet they were not only able to survive but thrive in an extremely dangerous time that required levels of SA far beyond what we are capable of doing today. So, what set them apart? Tools. In a hand to hand match you can't defeat a silver back gorilla however, with a spear in one to one combat you stand a greater chance. Now imagine humans hunting in parties or groups. They become vastly deadlier and vastly more cunning. Remember that the hands do not lie and when dealing with unknown persons it's critical to know at all times where their hands are.

Physical Cues

Now apply this to modern times. You are approached or you approach a suspicious person. Common curtesy and what your momma taught you dictates that you should look someone in the eye when you are talking to them. Though I would agree when meeting with family or conducting a business transaction I would whole heartedly disagree during a security situation. Watch the hands. Now say it with me, watch the hands. As I discussed earlier, humans use tools to commit the worst kinds of violence but let's start with if they don't have any tools. You are approached, you glance down at the person's hands, is there anything in them? No. Ok then, what is the demeanor of their hands. Are they calm and open, relaxed even? I hope so. If they ball up into a fist this is a clear sign of aggression and you need to keep your distance. What about shaking or trembling? This can be a sign of someone who is unstable or one form or another which puts them at greater odds of being physically aggressive. What about their pockets or waistline? Did you get a good look at those? While I live in Texas I tend to conceal carry a firearm in any state that will allow it, any other state that will allow it I always carry a knife. Is this person armed? And if so are they presenting any indicators that they will attack you?

A favorite saying of mine (and I hope it's an original one) is that good people are always ready for a fight, we just don't go looking for one. This essentially means that you should never assume that just because someone is armed that they are there to cause trouble or assault you. Be mindful of your state laws in regards to various tool carry laws. (Notice I did not call a firearm or knife a weapon. A person is the weapon. A firearm or knife can be used for various applications, often the least of which is taking a life) Once you have identified if they are armed or not you can continue to monitor the movement of their hands and their overall demeanor.

Let's move on to their face. Do they maintain eye contact? Those who plan on committing violence often maintain an uncomfortable level of eye contact. Their eyes will appear sharp, wide, with pupils constricted (small) as they focus on their target. Pupils that are dilated (large or normal in size) often describe one who is relaxed. What about their face? Is it relaxed or can you literally spot every wrinkle and crater therein? Are they sweating? Now keep in mind, if it's hot outside of course they would be sweating, however, if they are sweating disproportionally to the climate or time of day then either their heartbeat is elevated due to stress, adrenaline, or an underlying medical condition. Drugs could be a factor so don't rule out that the person you are interacting with may be under the influence of illicit substances or medications which would make them further unpredictable.

How about their torso? Are their arms and shoulders relaxed and at their sides? Or, are their shoulders up high, tense and perhaps their shoulders are pointed forward and hands slightly back? Tense shoulders will always communicate someone who is in an agitated state. If the hands are slightly behind the body this would be a cue for someone who is pulling back for a punch. What about their stance? This is an interesting one to point out as it differs greatly for everyone. If they are trained your SA needs to be aware that they will most likely take a bladed stance meaning they will either stand at a forty-five or ninety-degree angle which helps protect part of their body if they intend to attack you. The untrained, inebriated, or those who simply do not care will take a square stance, fists clenched, shoulders tensed, perhaps even their jaw clenched. Both are dangerous and require you to keep your distance. These are just some examples of physical cues and although there are probably many more I think that these will give you very real indicators if someone is an immediate threat or not.

Verbal Cues

Verbal cues that a person is a potential threat can be equally difficult to ascertain as physical cues. Some cues are very subtle and require and keen ear to understand them clearly, while others are quite plain. A person who is yelling or screaming at you is certainly a threat and is quite literally at the edge form becoming someone who is verbally attacking you to someone who is physically attacking you. It does not take much to cross that line but once the line is crossed it only takes a fraction of a second and now your ability to deescalate the situation has gone out the window. A direct threat is another clear verbal cue that someone is about to harm you. You need to keep that heightened level of SA. Some people will become too distracted with the person's emotions and forget to watch their body language that signals a coming attack. Examples of direct threats are, *I am going to kill you, I'll shoot you, I'll stab you*, etc. Pretty straight forward, right? Then there are indirect threats, these will require a certain level of listening, understanding or tone. An indirect may be, "If I don't get X I'm going to light this place up!" As you can see in the statement, the subject is making a threat that if they don't get something they want they are going to do something negative to some extent. They did not directly threaten you or I but made a broad statement of which we can't quite know what exactly the subject will do if the demands are not met. Another indirect threat I have heard often is, "You just wait and see…" in other words they want you to think of the worst possible thing they can do when the truth is probably that they will in fact do nothing.

Story Time

As I am writing this it was no more than two days ago that I had a very brief and violent interaction while on vacation and I think now would be a good time to share it and perhaps discuss some lessons learned.

My family and I were in Maui and had just arrived in Lahaina for a snorkeling tour. As we approached the docks my wife and mother-in-law needed to use the restroom. Naturally I waited outside for them and kept an eye on things as I did. I would describe my SA level at this point as fairly aware but certainly not heightened. As I waited for the ladies to return I surveyed my surroundings; there were at least a dozen homeless men wandering about and intermingled with tourist of every shape, size, and color. Within my immediate surroundings was one man wearing a straw hat, shorts, and carrying a bag as he walked back and forth talking to himself. Clearly this gentleman was a mental health case, under the influence of drugs, or both. Across the way, I heard a female vendor utter "You need to go away or I'm calling the cops." The man seemed to take some of this to heart and slowly made his way further towards the street and away from the docks. As he passed me I kept an eye on him and then when he left my sight I listened to the very unique sound of his flip flops dragging against concrete until they faded in the distance.

I felt in this moment that any immediate threats were gone and that my surroundings appeared clear and friendly. Then suddenly I heard a mumble behind me, I turned only to catch a glimpse of an angry face and then, bam! I will admit that it's been a while since I'd been punched in the face and I mean really punched, like someone swung a sack of quarters straight at your face kind of hit. I blacked out for a moment and stumbled and I was not immediately aware of what had happened. After two or three seconds the stars faded and I saw a man standing sixteen feet of so in front of me yelling in anger. His hands were empty, he wore a hat, a backpack, and my first thought was that he was on drugs or more than likely a mental health case. I had done nothing to offend the man but that didn't matter in this moment. What mattered was whether or not I was about to fight him. I stood upright and squared up against my opponent, he yelled louder, clenching his fists as he screamed at me. Then I took three steps forward to challenge him but the man fled.

The man was not ready for a fight. In fact, it appeared that his intention was to sucker punch me and knock me out cold so he could make away with the large bag I had wrapped around my neck and shoulder. It would make sense then why he attempted a surprise attack and then fled at the thought of a head-on encounter. He was looking for an easy target and perhaps a big reward. The bag I carried was rather large with our wallets, money, and credit cards inside along with a few expensive electronics for underwater photography. It would be safe to say he assumed something valuable was being carried. As the man ran off I gave a quick thought to chasing him but my family was still in the bathroom, they wouldn't know where I had gone if I needed help or got into trouble. Where would the assailant lead me? Would I end up in an alley or dead end where others would attempt to subdue me? Did he have weapons? I didn't know what was in his pockets or in his backpack. He could quickly produce a knife, gun, or improvised weapon (which the homeless often have) and I was unarmed and had no backup.

In light of these facts I let him go. I had won the fight and in some way deescalated the situation by being able to take a punch and stand my ground. It all made sense, logically, however my ego was terribly bruised. I wanted to tackle him to the ground and slam his face repeatedly into the ground while dropping blow after blow onto his head. I wanted revenge and I wanted him to pay for what he had done. It may have made my ego feel better to win in this manner but at the end of the day if I had done him serious injury or killed him I may be the one behind bars. The locals came to check on me afterward and repeatedly apologized as they did not want to actions of one Native Hawaiian to reflect on the whole island. They even called the cops for me and as predicted the Police arrived about six minutes after the incident occurred. A report was taken but I as asked the Officer a few questions in regards to prosecution and jail time it sounded as if Maui's very liberal laws would essentially let this guy go after he spent only a day in jail and most likely would be whisked away to a mental health facility before being released into the wild.

So, what did I learn here? Firstly, my SA was way too relaxed. I thought I had it covered, I thought I was watching the right guy but my head wasn't on a swivel and I never saw the real danger coming right up behind me. Despite being on vacation you should be ready for a fight at any time. Next was that I was unarmed, I left my knife back at the hotel because I was not planning on needing it while snorkeling; bad idea. I left myself unarmed and if the laws allow you to carry a knife, firearm, or other weapon you should take it upon yourself to do so. The one time you might need it is the one time you won't have it. Lastly, having a large bag on you makes you a target more so than anyone else who is not. One you are carrying goods you have now become an ideal opportunity for a criminal. Keep that in mind the next time you want to hit the town carrying bags upon bags of merchandise.

CHAPTER 4

Becoming Externally Aware

Do you remember the first time someone in your family had an emergency caused by something they had no control over? Perhaps it was something that originated hundreds of miles away that they simply did not know about. A hurricane is a great example. Do you watch the news? No? Well if you don't you should get started. The news provides a plethora of information, not the least of which is emergency external situations that may have an impact on you and your security operation. Does your site reside within the path of an oncoming storm? Do you have an Emergency Action Plan or EAP in place to address flooding or natural disaster events? First, I will discuss the types of incidents that you wanted to become externally aware of and then I will provide you some resources that can help you be externally aware.

Natural Disasters

Natural Disasters are by far the most common and most frequent event that impacts mankind as a civilization. If you watch news outlets it would have you believe that terrorism is in fact the worst but it's not so. Although terrorism is an awful occurrence that affects the lives of thousands every year it only impacts a fraction of those who are hard hit by natural disasters. What is a natural disaster? It is a natural phenomenon often weather or geological related that cause damage to property, injury to people and even death. On average, there are tens of millions of people impacted by natural disasters each and every year. The type of natural disasters varies but all of them have similar consequences.

- Blizzards

- Earthquakes

- Floods

- Hurricanes

- Landslides

- Tornadoes

- Wildfires

Each of the above named natural disasters have the capability to do untold damage to your site. It is therefore critical for you to understand what incidents you are most likely to experience at your site and identify how you and your site are prepared to address them. Emergency Action Plans or EAP's are often a great method of listing the steps you and your site would take in these emergencies. Without a plan in place your company may be ill equipped to respond and slow to react; by then of course, it's too late.

Terrorism/Organized Crime

Terrorism and Organized Crime is a nasty business and I could write volumes on the topic (many people have). Today when many hear the word terrorism they often immediately relate it to the middle east or Muslim extremism; but that is not an accurate definition. Terrorism is any group or organization of people who carry out violence or threats of violence with the aim of aiming political or religious goals. These individuals are found in nearly every country in all parts of the world often operating under different terms like "gangs", "mafias", or even "cartels". The names change but the meaning and their operations are essentially the same. The number one goal they all share is power and control over a geographical area and people. With today's world being as connected as it is many of these groups have become international by default. With modern technology and transportation these organizations have spread as far as their operations or competition will allow. For you the Security Professional it will be important to maintain SA on these groups that operate in your backyard. Though a rare occurrence for most Security Professionals you should be capable of recognizing the signs that they are actively in your Area of Operation or AO. Volumes and volumes of training have been created post 9/11 to educate Security professionals on these signs which I will cover in another lesson.

Disease/Pandemics

Though not normally impacting first world countries such as the United States of Europe it does happen. Two great examples are bird flu and swine flu. When swine flu became a problem in the United States I remember nearly every single staff member on our team becoming ill. Left and right Security Officers were calling in sick; dropping like flies and staying out of work for at least a week at a time. Daily work schedules of sixteen hours or more became common and for those of us who did not become ill we certainly became worn out.

I can still remember the constant smell hand sanitizer, the daily screening of security teams for any symptoms of sickness, wearing gloves and masks while on duty. The site I managed at the time became a ghost town as many employees who were sick worked from home and those not ill opted to work from home just to avoid coming into contact with others. It was a strange reality that brought up visions of the movie "Outbreak". It was always in the news and as usual the news did what they did best, they sensationalized the story and made everything seem much, much worse than it actually was. After three weeks passed everyone started slowly funneling back to the office and eventually everything went to normal. We fine-tuned our pandemic response plans based on hands on experience and packed away the many boxes of gloves, masks, and sanitizer we had on hand. The news of course milked the story for several more weeks.

In terms of SA for disease and pandemic events you can either avoid areas impacted or you can better prepare locations that are likely to be directly impacted. Self SA is critical as well; what are you doing to prevent disease? Did you get your most recent flu shot? Are you eating healthy and exercising? Are you cleaning and sanitizing workspaces properly to avoid cross-contamination? What about your home? If you have kids like me, you know they are always the first ones to get sick because they spend hours in the incubator of disease called school. All of those kids picking their nose, scratching at everything and contracting every possible childhood sickness to build up their immune system. Then they come home…and you get sick… every…single…time.

Geopolitical Events

Geopolitical events are equally as important but occur less frequently than the above named incidents. What is a geopolitical event? It is any situation that impacts nations internally or externally that can have negative consequences. An age-old example is North Korea. Since the end of the Korean War we have danced with North Korea over and over again regarding their dictatorship and their constant threats to their neighbor, the free and beautiful South Korea. This geopolitical situation costs millions upon millions of dollars each year to manage and maintain in order to ensure that the totalitarian rule of the North does not conquer the South. A similar situation has brewed in recent years with the reemergence of the Soviet Union who in many ways is attempting to recapture their former glory as the U.S.S.R. With a portion of Ukraine now firmly occupied and controlled by the Soviet Union tensions in the eastern block of Europe have now flared up to Cold War proportions. Soviet bombers and fighter jets have once again taken to the skies and on a regular basis invade American airspace in an effort to flex their muscles. This has created unique geopolitical situations that can impact a Security Professional and the level of SA required for a particular AO. However, not all geopolitical situations are purely based on war or the threat of war. Some situations are purely political and place a strain on a country internally. Take the United Kingdom for example; BREXIT or British Exit from the European Union created a massive rift within British culture and the people took to the streets to protest both against and in favor for the historic move. Though I will attempt to avoid my own opinion on the matter I can firmly say that to decision to exit which the voters clearly decided upon was firmly based on the overwhelmingly level of tax and bureaucracy inflicted upon them by the centralized control of the Germans, not to mention the unbridled and uncontrolled immigration of peoples from worn torn countries in the middle-east which led to unprecedented levels of terrorism from within the UK. The people were worn and tired and they made their decision.

For the Security Professional BREXIT poses unique challenges both internally and externally. Internally it must be difficult to have any communication around the topic as many are so feverously passionate about it. Having the "perceived wrong opinion" on the matter can get one on the bad end of Human Resources or worse yet, fired. That's right, I said it, fired, sacked, terminated, removed. Companies have "cultures" and if you don't fit the culture you are often not hired or if the culture shifts you are eventually removed in some way, shape, or form. With this in mind, be measured with the things you say and whom you say them to. Freedom of speech is guaranteed by the U.S. Constitution but it will not protect you from your company letting you go. In terms of external concerns, depending upon where you work, the type of company, or its geographic location you may be more exposed to these types of protest incidents which may cause property damage or physical damage to those whom support the opposition. Be aware, keep you SA high, and never drop your guard.

CHAPTER 5

The Mindset

If you've stuck with me this far you are now in the last chapter and I want to thank you for your attention and dedication. I hope that so far, I've been able to give you some tools that you can utilize not just on duty but skills for life in general. My last point I wanted to address with you the Security Professional was the mindset in regards to SA. Those that operate at very low levels of SA are not bad people, they are just simply "SA Unaware". Now, I would think that if someone was virtually SA Unaware that this would place them at risk for an early death because every single one of us no matter what profession we are in or if we are just a stay at home parent (which is an extremely difficult job by the way) or a single person we can all run into situations that we want to avoid. We don't want to be in fatal car crashes, we don't want to die falling down the stairs, and we don't want to get run over by a car just by crossing the street. I think that every human being must be capable, and they are, of a basic level of SA. Now let's talk about the complete other spectrum, someone who is extremely SA Aware.

The Security Professional who is on the extreme side of SA operating at an extremely high level has little time for side conversations, jokes, or employee development. They are focused at the mission at hand 110% of the time. Now, depending on the type of job they are doing this could be a good or a bad thing. If you are working a Physical Security Detail or PSD in Iraq or Afghanistan than you are operating exactly at the level you should. However, if you try to take this level to say a standing guard post in the lobby of a Corporate Financial Institution I hate to tell you but your overall "perceived" attitude will not fly. How will they perceive you? Well to be frank, like an asshole. That's right, I said it. They will look at you like you are a complete and utter asshole, a jackass, someone screwed so tight that no amount of WD-40 could loosen them up.

First and foremost, the physical security industry is a customer service business. *Wait a minute, what?* You heard me right, the physical security industry is a customer service business. We are hired by clients not only for protection but to create friendly "security theater". Your high level of SA and the completely serious look on your face will make you completely and utterly unapproachable. Executive Admins will complain about you, those sensitive to authority figures will find you overly intimidating and sales professionals will think you are a joke. Why you may ask? Well, this is because the majority of these professionals have never worked in the military, law enforcement, or the physical security industry. Their preconceived notions of what security should be, is based on stereotypes and the movie "Paul Blart: Mall Cop". It's sad but true. If only they knew that the physical security industry is multi-billion-dollar industry that literally saves the lives of tens or thousands of citizens each year and mitigates the loss of hundreds of billions of dollars if not more in company assets and proprietary information.

It is difficult to sometimes quantify the return on investment corporations receive from the security companies they higher but the longer I work in this industry the more I realize that we are always underpaid, undermanned, and undervalued. So, how do we combat some of these realities? How do we win over those who have no concept of why our SA is so high and why we act the way that we do? With a smile. That's it. A smile and an overall friendly demeanor can get you far in life. *But what about the guy who never smiles and has his finger constantly in his ear looking like a tough guy?* Well, that guy is doing a very particular job at the moment which you can do to, but when those jobs are over and your back to finding your next client or doing something that's not so "high-speed" you will inevitably be working with normal people. It's time to slightly lower that SA and raise your friendly demeanor. A conversation I have had many times is, why can't we have both? Why can't we operate at extreme levels of SA but still be approachable? Well, to be honest, it's just difficult. It took me years to "deprogram" from my U.S. Marine Corps persona.

Teaching Situational Awareness

Have you ever had someone tell you that you're too paranoid? Yeah, me too. It's something my wife used to tell me all the time. Then as she got to hear my many stories over the years she finally understood why I would always reply saying, *I'm not paranoid, I'm cautious.* I've found the military and law enforcement personnel are certainly a different breed when it comes to SA and it's true. When they transition to the Physical Security Industry many people they interact with will feel that they are paranoid, too serious, or perhaps they came down with PTSD while in their previous career. Although some people are impacted by traumatic events like PTSD or some other form of anxiety due to repeated exposure to stressful situations, those with a heightened state of SA act and hold themselves in a different manner which often separates them from those who do not carry these traits. But I digress, those who have this level of SA need to be capable of teaching other in the industry.

Coming across as too serious or even mean will make you un-relatable and most people will be turned off by the idea of having to learn anything from you. To start, teach your staff to be overly cautious as I call it. Give them examples of how normal people would often ignore a smell, noise, a drip of water and then explain how these small items ignored could turn into something much bigger, perhaps even fatal. A strange odor could be a gas leak, an odd sound could be someone breaking into your facility or it could be someone having a heart attack unable to call for help, the drip of water could be a much larger flooded upstairs which would soon break through the ceiling. The average person without an elevated SA level will not recognize the signs that lead to disaster and therefore it is up to you, the Security Professional, to read between the lines and find chaos in things that no one else would. Your intuition and gut instinct could be all that stands in the way of a life and death situation.

I'll give you another parody from which to compare. Ancient humans, otherwise known as Neanderthals were a wild people. They lived in the wild, they slept in the wild, they foraged in the wild and they fought for their lives in the wild. Every broken blade of grass or scent on the wind was a kind of sign or signal that either danger was near or the animals they were hunting were not far off. The level of SA that a Neanderthal had to attain was far beyond what any of us could experience. Even todays soldiers that survive the trials of war eventually come home and the environment they are in no longer requires a completely heightened level of SA. No, the Neanderthal was constantly on alert, ready at a moment's notice to fight off fearsome ice age predators like the saber tooth tiger or team combat neighboring clans seeking to take their lives and assets. But just like the Neanderthal or the soldier in a combat zone, we can create a baseline for what is and what is not normal. A leak in a building, no matter how small is not normal. A sudden loud noise in a manufacturing facility after hours is not normal. An unknown small wafting in an office where before there was none is not normal. Teach your officers to be suspicious and overly cautious.

How "Not" to Teach Situational Awareness

One time I managed a Security Unit for a Sheriff's department. It was a very large program with hundreds of Security Officers and multiple facilities spread over a fairly large geographic area. One of these facilities was a large rural airport that hosted some fairly prestigious clients of the bay area. One of my jobs as the new security manager was to evaluate and test the current level of security at these locations. So, I did just that. One early morning at about 0300 hours I rolled up on the airport with my vehicle lights turned off and parked under the darkness of a tree. I exited my vehicle and began surveying the property where I located the "one" security officer for the entire airport who conducted patrols in a vehicle from one end of the airport to the other. As I observed their movements for an hour or so the patrols and length of time at vary locations became painfully predictable. I waited for my twenty-minute window until the guard had passed be by unnoticed. I then jumped over the six-foot fence and proceed to walk by a multitude of aircraft, hangars, etc., snapping close up pictures of each aircraft to show proof of where I had been and how close I came to each. After thirty minutes or so of wandering about the airfield undetected the Security Officer patrol was coming back around right on schedule. I crept back into the shadows and waited for the guard to predictably pass by, which they did. Then I moved on to testing the security of the many gates at this airfield.

There were dozens of the gates, each one controlled by a simple keypad that would allow client to drive straight onto the airfield and to their hangars. The gates were secure enough, although I am adamantly opposed to keypad locks, simply because the codes tend to get passed around too often and are rarely changed. Not to mention the height of the gates were not adequate to even keep out the most random offender. From the inside of the gates I was able to open them manually and so I took very small pebbles placing them in front of the locking mechanism. The gates appeared shut to the average eye, what I wanted to know was whether or not the Security Officer would notice. After placing pebbles in several gates, I returned to my vehicle in the shadows and patiently waited for the guard to return for inspections. As expected and right on schedule, they did. One by one the Security Officer inspected the gates and one by one it seemed that my intrusion had been unnoticed until with the fourth gate the security officer saw the pebble drop from the gate. She looked around curiously and then immediately moved on to check the others where she slowly opened them without using a code and in each instance noticed the pebble fall to the ground. She raised her radio and contacted the Police. In five minutes or so, six squad cars arrived on scene. I slowly exited my vehicle and approached the Officers explaining to them who I was and what had occurred. The Officers were not happy and returned to their patrol. The Lieutenant and the Sergeant that I reported into who were both aware of my activities were happy to hear about the Police response but obviously disappointed with the lack of security at this previously presumed "secure" location. After everything was said and done and plans were in place to write a formal security survey and recommendations I met with the Security Officer at the airport. She was not happy. The guard was now in fear for their job, overwhelmed with embarrassment and frankly angry that we had not met previously to discuss that I would be conducting these drills. There was now a serious lack of trust and quite honestly, I was unable to establish any trust with that Officer going forward. As a manager, I failed to build an environment of trust with this employee, in fact, in the name of SA I literally threw this employee under the bus. Eventually they resigned from their job. It was an unfortunate turn of events, and when I thought I was working towards improving our teams SA I actually blindsided one of my own. So, what advice would I give now?

Always conduct scenario training with your team prior conducting live drills. This will ensure that you have already evaluated the gaps with the team and together improve the program prior to testing. Secondly, always give your team a time range of when a live scenario may happen. A week is usually sufficient enough. This keeps them on their toes longer and nobody really knows what's going to happen. This increases their SA level and helps them hone those skills as they prepare mentally and physically for a potential intrusion.

Avoiding Burnout

Let's face it, we all need a time out from time to time. A vacation or perhaps just a long weekend to unwind. You can't constantly be at the top of your SA game. Just like your endurance during a run, eventually you will wear out. Taking the time for yourself to relax and refocus is critical. Personally, I prefer getting away from people or situations that would activate my SA instincts. I don't like malls anymore, there's too many people, too many noises and too much going on. In general, I don't really like any place that is crowded. It puts me on alert and makes me feel like I have to keep watch over everyone and what they are doing. I'm not going to lie, it's hard to turn the switch off after so many years. My inner peace is found camping, fishing, in the woods or quite simply in my backyard. Luckily, I happen to live in a quiet neighborhood and kicking back with a beer and some meat on the grill is often my recipe to recharge. Then there are the adrenaline junkies, those who have to take it up a notch just to feel normal. I get that to, I still play hockey and slamming guys body against the wall while causing myself some physical pain is often a great stress relief mechanism. Just find what works for you and be sure to schedule some time to do those things.

I've met many Security Professionals who never take a day off. These are the guys constantly chugging red bull or monster energy drinks and often pick up bad habits like smoking or chewing tobacco. Besides the negative health side effects of some of these items I really would not recommend any of them but back to my point: take your vacation. The Security Professionals who don't take their vacation become less and less effective as the months go by. At one point or another, they snap, whether it's yelling at subordinates or taking it out on their family. Take, your, vacation.

In Closing

I want to thank you for taking the time to read my take and the take of other professionals on situational awareness. I wish that I had this kind of knowledge and guidance when I started in the industry. Now that I'm making it available to you I hope that it will serve you well and perhaps carry you throughout your career. Just like exercise, SA is something you must work on every day of your life if you hope to become any good at it. The more often you become lax or lazy and fail to follow a regimen of some kind the weaker your SA will become. If you are already feeling burnt out, stressed, or overworked; even working in one of my SA building techniques could help improve your job performance and your quality of life.

REFERENCES

Author: Department of Homeland Security
Page Title: Situational Awareness
Site Title: United States Coast Guard
Date last revised: Unknown
Date accessed: 9/1/2017
URL
https://www.uscg.mil/auxiliary/training/tct/chap5.pdf

Author: National Imagery and Mapping Agency
Title: Report Writing Guidelines for Incident Report Writing
Pages Used: 2
City: Duncan, OK
Publisher: APTAC
Copyright Date: 2009
URL
http://police-praetorian.netdna-ssl.com/pdfs/reportwritingmanual.pdf

Author: Bureau of Labor Statistics
Page Title: Security Guards, Injuries, Illnesses, and Fatalities
Site Title: Bureau of Labor Statistics
Date last revised: June 2009
Date accessed: 3/12/2015
URL
http://www.bls.gov/iif/oshwc/osh/os/osar0009.pdf

Author: Bureau of Labor Statistics
Page Title: Occupational Employment and Wages, May 2013
Site Title: Bureau of Labor Statistics
Date last revised: May 2013
Date accessed: 3/12/2015
URL http://www.bls.gov/oes/current/oes339032.htm

Author: Bureau of Labor Statistics

Page Title: Occupational Outlook Handbook, Security Guards and Gaming Surveillance Officers
Site Title: Bureau of Labor Statistics
Date last revised: Jan. 8th, 2014
Date accessed: 3/12/2015
URL
http://www.bls.gov/ooh/protective-service/security-guards.htm

Author: Department of Consumer Affairs
Title: Power to Arrest Training Manual
Pages Used: 4,5,17
City: State of California
Publisher: Department of Consumer Affairs
Copyright Date: 10/2011
URL
http://www.bsis.ca.gov/forms_pubs/poa.pdf

Author: National Imagery and Mapping Agency
Title: International Code of Signals
Pages Used: 18
City: United States of America
Publisher: International Code of Signals
Copyright Date: 2003, United States Government

Author: The Library of Congress
Title: The Pinkertons
City: United States of America
Publisher: The Library of Congress
Copyright Date: 01/2011
URL
http://memory.loc.gov/ammem/today/aug25.html

Author: The Roman Curia
Title: Swiss Guard History
City: The Vatican
Publisher: The Vatican

Copyright Date: N/A
URL
http://www.vatican.va/roman_curia/swiss_guard/swissguard/storia_en.l

Author: United States Marine Corps
Title: International Rifle Marksmanship
Pages Used: 3-1, 3-2
City: United States of America
Publisher: Department of the Navy
Copyright Date: 1999, United States Government

Author: John Ellery
Title: Radio Communication for Security
City: N/A
Publisher: Security Solutions Magazine
Copyright Date: May 2, 2012
URL
http://www.securitysolutionsmagazine.biz/2012/05/02/radio-
communication-for-security/

Author: Robert D. Sollars
Title: Cultivating and Improving Situational Awareness Among Your
Security Officers
City: N/A
Publisher: SilverTrac
Copyright Date: September 25, 2015
URL
https://www.silvertracsoftware.com/extra/cultivating-and-improving-
situational-awareness-among-your-security-officers